God Is With Us – Everywhere!

A Rhyming Nativity Play

Suitable for live or virtual performance

by

Fay Rowland

Copyright

Visit the author's website at www.fayrowland.co.uk

Typeset in Century Gothic 11pt.

ISBN: 9798691445224

Using This Script

Acknowledgements

My grateful thanks, as always, to my children for putting up with a mum who is always going 'tappity, tappity, tap' on the keyboard and forcing them to eat pizza for tea. (Not sure that they mind, really.)

Thanks also to my venerable proof-reader, Steve D, and to all those who have given constructive criticism on this and other projects.

Enormous thanks to my friend and mentor Ally B for her wonderful artwork and word-smithing. You'll find snippets of her artwork on the cover and scattered around, ensuring that the sections start on the correct-facing pages and beautifying what would otherwise be blank spaces. Her Christmas Sonnet is printed at the end of this book for a quiet moment of festive reflection.

Thank you, finally, to those who support my writing ministry at The Reflectionary. The resources there are given away for free because I believe this stuff is important, but I do still need to make a living! If you have not visited yet, may I encourage you to pop along to www.reflectionary.org?

By buying this book you are helping me to continue so, for being part of the team, gentle reader, THANK YOU! You're a star!

(That's always assuming you've actually bought this book. If you haven't, why not?)

God Is With Us – Everywhere!

A Rhyming Nativity Play

Cast

This drama is especially designed to accommodate a varied number of participants. Whether you have a small Sunday school or you need to find parts for an entire classful of children, this drama can cope. You could even run it in a family, if you are happy to double up on parts.

There are nine named characters plus a narrator (who could be an adult) so the minimum is 9 + 1, but with the addition of non-speaking parts and splitting the narrator's lines, you could have thirty or more people taking part.

Character	Number of verses
Narrator	33 (you can split this role)
Gabriel	11
Mary	9
Joseph	7
Amos (shepherd)	3
Seth (shepherd)	3
Colin (apprentice shepherd)	3
Melchior (wise man)	3
Gaspar (wise man)	3
Balthazar (wise man)	3

Casting

Although angels are often thought of as girls' roles, in the Bible, angels are male, and can be scary!

Gabriel in this play is not a cutesy little girl with blond pigtails. You might consider casting a tough-looking boy who can carry off the comedy section when he realises he has scared Mary. Gabriel has the largest speaking part after the Narrator(s).

For other parts, Mary and Joseph should be a girl and a boy, but all the other characters could be played by anyone.

Non-speaking parts

If you wish to include younger children, you can add as many non-speaking parts as you like.

Children can dress up as donkeys, cows or any other farm animal for scene 3, as angels or sheep for scene 4, or as camels or stars for scene 5.

For in-person performances, they can sit along the front or stand up in their places during the appropriate scenes.

For virtual performances, each one can record a short video making an appropriate noise ('moo', 'baa', 'twinkle'). You can insert these between the spoken verses for maximum cute appeal.

Narrator(s)

The Narrator has 33 verses to speak in total, so you may wish to share this role among several people. There are different ways to do this, depending on how many people you want to include:

- A single Narrator can read all the verses
  1 narrator, total cast = 10

- You could have a small team (eg, 4) taking the verses in turns
  4 taking turns, total cast = 13

- You could have a different Narrator for each scene
  6 narrators, total cast = 15

- You could have small teams for each scene, taking the verses in turns
  2 taking turns for each scene, total cast = 21
  3 taking turns for each scene, total cast = 27

The reflective section at the end of scene 5 has the Narrator(s) speaking six consecutive verses. If you are performing in person, the wise men could sit down for this part, so that the focus is on the Narrators.

Narrators should be confident readers, but do not need to learn their lines. Their words can be printed out in large type and placed inside a Bible. The narrators then appear to be reading the Bible story (albeit slightly paraphrased!)

Costume Suggestions and Props

You can use traditional or modern costumes, or a mixture of both.

Narrator(s)	Christmas jumper and tinsel
Gabriel	Jeans, shades and leather jacket, or traditional white robe, plus halo and wings
Mary	Traditionally wears blue with head drape
Joseph	Construction worker or Joseph costume
Amos	Farmer or shepherd costume, with beard
Seth	Farmer or shepherd costume, with beard
Colin	Farmer or shepherd costume, no beard
Melchior	Scientist or wise man costume
Gaspar	Scientist or wise man costume
Balthazar	Scientist or wise man costume

Props

- Mary and Joseph need phones.
- Joseph needs a letter.
- Mary needs a wallet or credit card.
- Mary can also have a cushion for a 'bump'.
- Colin needs a sheep or some 'wool' (eg cushion stuffing).
- Balthazar needs a book or chart of stars.
- All wise men need gifts.

Everyone (including Narrators) needs a doll wrapped in a white blanket for baby Jesus in the last scene. These should be kept hidden until noted in the script.

Staging

The script is divided into six scenes. You can spread them throughout a service, with songs and readings between, or you can run them back-to-back for a continuous story.

Staging – in person

If you are using separate scenes, the characters for each scene can stand spaced out across the front with the narrator(s) at the sides. The characters can return to their classes or families after each scene.

If you are running all the scenes together, you may prefer to have the characters stay with their families or classes throughout. They can stand on their chairs in place to speak, scattered throughout the room. You will need to make sure that the acoustics are good enough so that they can be heard.

Staging – virtual

This play has been designed to work for worship where people cannot gather together. In this situation, the title is especially poignant: *God Is With Us – Everywhere!*

Each character should record their lines separately, starting a new video when a new person speaks. You can combine the clips one after another, trimming the ends, to make the final video. It looks good to have a photo of each person holding their Jesus doll and combine these into one image for the opening and closing titles.

For the final verse you can make a video mosaic if you have that technology, or use the mosaic photo over everyone saying the last verse. If that is too tricky, have the narrator say those lines instead.

Hints and Tips

All the verses have the same rhythm as 'Tinker, Tailor, Soldier, Sailor':

DUM dee DUM dee DUM dee DUM dee
DUM dee DUM dee DUM dee DUM

This is to help people remember their lines, and to keep a steady flow, but characters should not sound too 'clumpy' or mechanical when they speak.

It very, VERY much helps if characters can learn their lines, especially when filming videos, when they only have to learn the lines for one section at a time.

For videos, make sure the lighting is even, and make sure that _everyone films in landscape mode_!

The word in square brackets and italics [like this] are stage directions. Do them, don't read them out!

Characters and Scenes

Narrator	1, 2, 3, 4, 5, 6
Gabriel	1, 2, 4, 6
Mary	1, 2, 3, 6
Joseph	2, 3, 6
Amos (shepherd)	4, 6
Seth (shepherd)	4, 6
Colin (apprentice shepherd)	4, 6
Melchior (wise man)	5, 6
Gaspar (wise man)	5, 6
Balthazar (wise man)	5, 6

God Is With Us – Everywhere!

The Script

Scene 1 At Mary's Home

Narr   Welcome to our Christmas story,
          we re-tell it every year:
          How God came from heaven's glory,
          came to make his home right here.

          Jesus, lying in a manger,
          born in all our mess and fuss,
          made us friends who once were strangers,
          Son of God who lives with us.

          Soon we'll meet the shepherds, wisemen,
          all the usual Christmas crew
          and, perhaps, another story -
          one that's now involving you.

          In our world of joy and darkness,
          in our laughter, pain and care,
          Jesus came so we could know that
          God Is With Us – Everywhere!
              [spreading arms wide]

          So our story starts as always
          with an angel, Gabriel,
          visiting the home of Mary.
          Was she busy? Who can tell?
              [shrugging shoulders]

Mary   *[sweeping busily]*
            All today I'm cooking, sweeping,
            feed the chickens, knead the dough.
            [miming jobs]
            Honestly, it's never-ending!
            Time to sit down for a mo.
            [sitting down, looking tired]

Narr   But as soon as Mary rested
            someone knocked upon her door.
            [make knocking sound]
            Grumpily she went to answer,
            not expecting what she saw.

Gab   *[looking impressive, with loud voice]*
            Greetings, Mary, highly favoured.
            I have come to you from God
            with a message straight from heaven.
            [in a normal voice]
            Oh! You look a little odd.

            Yes, I realise you're frightened,
            seems to happen quite a lot.
            People see the wings and halo –
            gives them all a nasty shock!

            [concerned and caring]
            Would you like a glass of water?
            Do sit down dear, there's a love.
            That's much better. Here's the message
            I have brought from God above.
            [clearing throat, ready to start again]

Narr   Gabriel explained to Mary
          God had chosen her to be
          mother of a special baby –
          God's gift for humanity!

Mary   *[looking confused]*
          Ummn, don't want to seem ungrateful,
          but there's just one tiny thing
          I should mention, just in passing.
          See my hand? No wedding ring!
              *[showing both sides of left hand, like in the
          song 'Single Ladies']*

Gab   Mary, don't get all Beyoncé!
          It's OK, the child will be
          not the son of your fiancé,
          but of God, the one in three.
              [fingers showing 1 then 3]

          Father God will send his Spirit
          and become the Holy Son.
          So the child you'll bear will be the
          Son of God, the three in one.
              [fingers showing 3 then 1]

Mary   Wow! That's quite a thing you're asking,
          God himself will come to stay?
          But I am the Lord God's servant.
          Let it happen as you say.
              [bowing slightly, hands in prayer shape]

Narr   So the angel bowed and left her.
          Mary sat and drank some tea,
              [miming drinking tea]
          called up her fiancé, Joseph.
          What would his reaction be?
              [shrugging shoulders]

Scene 2   Joseph and the Angel

Narr   Right across the town from Mary
       Joseph had a wood-work shop.
       He was busy making benches
       when a phone call made him stop.

Joseph   [answering phone]
         Joseph here, all tables mended,
         doors and windows, fences too.
             [looking proud]
         Carpenter to all of Naz'reth.
         Who's there? Mary? Oh, it's you!

Mary   [talking on phone]
         Joseph dear, I've news to tell you:
         we are going to have a child.
         God's own son, an angel told me.
             [looking worried]
         Now, please Joseph, don't get riled.

Joseph   [looking shocked and sad]
         Mary, this is disappointing.
         Not that I am mad or cross,
         but I must do what is righteous.
             [shaking head]
         Sorry, but the wedding's off.
             [putting phone down and sighing]

Narr   Joseph planned to do this quietly,
caring still for Mary's plight.
Gabriel had news for Joseph
In a dream, that very night.

Gabriel   *[hands round mouth, calling]*
Joseph, son of David, listen!
You are frightened. That's OK.
    [thumbs up]
It's alright to marry Mary,
you'll still have your wedding day.

Mary said the babe she's bearing
is from God, and that is right.
Call him Jesus (which means saviour).
He will be this dark world's light.

Narr   Joseph made it up with Mary
and they set a wedding day,
but before they picked the bridesmaids
something happened – Ah! Oy Vey!
    ['Oy Vey!' is a Jewish phrase like 'Oh no!']

Joseph   *[waving letter]*
Mary, I've just got this letter.
Not good news, cos it's from *Them*
(you know, Romans), 'bout our taxes.
Time to pay - in Bethlehem!

Mary   *[looking shocked]*
              What? You mean we've got to travel
              while I'm pregnant? That's too hard.
              Can't we pay by direct debit,
              Visa Pay or Mastercard?
                    [waving wallet or card]

Joseph   *[shrugging shoulders]*
              Sorry sweetie, not invented.
              It is Bethlehem or bust.
              I'll start packing. Put your feet up.
              Comfy footwear – that's a must.

Scene 3 By the Manger

Narr   So to Bethlehem they travelled,
('cos of Joseph's family tree)
walked for days and days to get there.
Were they tired? Guess we'll see.
[shrugging shoulders]

Joseph   *[walking on the spot]*
Nearly there now, Mary darling,
won't be long till supper time.
We can stay with Bob, my uncle,
in his guest-room, you'll be fine.

Mary   *[walking on the spot, leaning backwards]*
Really hope so, Joseph dearest.
Baby's nearly on his way.
When we get there, call the midwife.
Think you'll be a dad today!
[patting tummy]

Narr   Uncle Bob had made it lovely
but the room was very small.
Mary much preferred it downstairs,
just beside the donkey's stall.

So that night, as stars were twinkling
Mary's tiny babe was born.
Joseph filled the donkey's trough with
hay and blankets, soft and warm.

Joseph   [picking up baby Jesus doll]
         Can I hold him? Will he like me?
         Do you think he'll call me 'Dad'?
         [eeew!]
         God's own son just wet his nappy.
         Mary, dear, you're looking sad.
         [noticing Mary]

Mary   [looking at baby Jesus doll]
         I was thinking, will he be a
         carpenter like you, you reckon?
         Making chairs and tables, or does
         something very diff'rent beckon?

         [wondering]
         Will he grow to be like you, or
         will he take his Father's job?
         Nestling in your arms I see the
         face of human, soul of God.

Narr   As they gazed in awe and wonder
         at their baby, sleeping sound,
            [looking around and above]
         silently, beyond their vision,
         all of heaven gathered round.

         God no longer just in glory,
         but right here where humans dwell.
            [opening arms wide to include everybody]
         God made flesh to be God With Us,
         Jesus, our Emmanuel.
            [bringing hands together to present baby]

Scene 4 Shepherds and Angels

Narr   Meanwhile, on a distant hillside
shepherds sat there, tending sheep
Amos, Seth, apprentice Colin
round the campfire, half asleep.
[yawning]

[suddenly awake]
All at once they heard some singing,
saw a brilliant shining light.
Gabriel arrived in glory.
[looking scared]
What a terrifying sight!

Amos   *[looking up, scared]*
What the flippin' 'eck is 'happenin'?
Seth and Colin, wake up now!
Aliens, I think, or Martians!
Don't look at 'em! Hit the ground!
[lying flat on face]

Gab   *[apologetic]*
Sorry, didn't mean to scare you
(it's the halo, I suppose),
but I have some information.
'Scuse me while I strike a pose.

[in 'hero' pose]
Do not fear, I bring glad tidings!
News of joy for all the earth.
News about a special baby.
News about a new king's birth.

Seth   Get up off the ground there Amos!
       There's no need to hide your face.
           [doing 'face-palm']
       Martians? It's a bloomin' angel,
       not some dude from outer space!

Colin   *[pointing upwards, amazed]*
       Look, there's loads now, singing "Glory,
       glory be to God on high.
       Peace on Earth to everybody."
       Angels filling all the sky.

Gab   *[pointing sideways]*
       Hurry now to David's city,
       Bethlehem, and you will see
       wrapped in cloth and in a manger,
       Lord of all eternity.

           [slight pause]
           [in normal voice, not in rhythm]
       Get a move on then!
       Don't just stand there gawping.

Narr   So the shepherds left the hillside,
       and, just off the city square,
       found the house with Mary, Joseph
       and the baby lying there.

Amos   *[beaming]*
            Ain't he lovely? Who'd have thought it?
            Me, old Amos, standing here,
            right before the Lord of Glory!
            Makes me knees come over queer.
                [wobbling knees]

Seth   *[scratching head]*
            Feel I should have brought a present.
            Could not think of what to bring.
            What could shepherds give a baby
            Lord of lords and King of kings?

Colin   *[showing wool (cushion stuffing) or sheep]*
            I brought wool for him to sleep on,
            comfier than straw and hay.
                [sniffing wool / sheep]
            Smells of sheep I know, but this is
            from the heart. Is that OK?
                [offering wool / sheep]

Narr   So the shepherds knelt and worshipped,
                [looking down then looking up]
            feet on Earth and eyes on heaven.
            Jesus slept and snuggled softly
            on the wool that they had given.

Sure, it had no fancy wrapping.
    [shaking head]
Ribbons? None, nor sparkly bow.
But the gift they gave to Jesus
    [nodding]
came with love instead of show.

So, as Colin, Seth and Amos
went back to their dozing sheep,
Jesus somehow went there with them,
giving _presence_ they could keep.

Scene 5 Wise Men Visit

Narr   Later on, a group of wise men
        travelled in from lands afar.
        Scientists, we'd call them these days,
        following a bright new star.
            [pointing and looking upwards to star]

Mel   [riding on camel (pretend, obviously)]
        Are we nearly there yet, Gaspar?
        We've been travelling for weeks.
        Can you just remind me why we've
        come, and what it is we seek?

Gas   Melchior, have you forgotten?
        Honestly, you noodle-brain!
            [showing gift]
        We bring gifts to greet and welcome,
        celebrate a new king's reign.

Bal   [pointing to book or chart]
        All our books and all our wisdom,
        told us that this star so bright
        means that king and God and saviour
        will be born this very night.

Narr   When the wise men stopped their journey
         what they found was quite a shock:
         Mary, Joseph, babe in manger,
         shepherds outside with their flock.

Mel   Can I check, this *is* the right place?
         I brought gold to crown a king,
              [presenting gift]
         but I wonder, where's the palace?
         Is this manger quite the thing?

Gas   I brought incense, pure and holy,
         made to worship God on high.
              [presenting gift]
         Is this baby, weak and helpless
         Mighty God with human cry?

Bal   I brought myrrh, which symbolises
         one who dies to save us all.
              [presenting gift]
         Seems a strange gift for a baby,
         job too big for one so small.

Narr   So the wise men gave their presents
         though they did not understand
         how the child who lay before them
         would, one day, give this command:

"Follow me!", he'd call to many,
preach Good News in all he said,
heal the sick and free the captives.
Would they follow where he led?

Gave his life to pay our ransom,
bought us all at costly price.
Righteous king and God and saviour.
Perfect lamb as sacrifice.

Raised to life to raise us with him,
Victor, Christ and Living Word.
All this lay before the baby
sleeping soundly, undisturbed.

So the wise men knelt around him,
gave their costly presents, then
suddenly, they knew that they'd be
taking treasure home with them.

Richer than the purest incense,
costlier than gold or myrrh,
wise men took home truest Wisdom,
Prince of Peace and Comforter.

Scene 6 God Is With Us

Narr Now our story's almost ended.
Everyone has met him here.
Will you take the Christmas baby
home with you throughout the year?

Let us hear from all the people
who have met with God today.
How will this affect their stories?
Will this change them? Who can say?
[shrugging shoulders]

Mary Strangest night, but stranger morning.
Joy and sadness like a sword.
When I kiss my baby's forehead
I believe I kiss my Lord.
[Hold up Jesus doll]

Joseph Though I'm his adopted father
I will raise him as my son,
teach him all I know and love him,
serve my King 'til kingdom come.
[Hold up Jesus doll]

Amos I don't really understand it,
all the stuff the angels said,
but I know I knelt and worshipped
by the Lord Almighty's bed.
[Hold up Jesus doll]

Seth   Why would God come down to shepherds,
        poorest folk of all the poor?
        Live with us and make us worthy
        I don't know, but I adore.
        [Hold up Jesus doll]

Colin   What have I to give to Jesus?
        Nothing, but yet everything.
        All my heart and soul and worship,
        for the baby, God and king.
        [Hold up Jesus doll]

Mel   Gold I brought, expecting royals,
        Majesty I found instead.
        Higher King than all kings ever,
        lying in a manger bed.
        [Hold up Jesus doll]

Gas   I brought incense, made for worship,
        rising as a prayer to heaven.
        Prayers now answered by the baby,
        God's own gift to me is given.
        [Hold up Jesus doll]

Bal   Myrrh I brought, not understanding
        how this babe would die and live,
        bringing life in all its fullness –
        gifts that only he could give.
        [Hold up Jesus doll]

Gab   So God's plan before creation,
       Earth in heaven and heaven on Earth,
       came in form of gentle baby,
       Mighty God in human birth.
           [Hold up Jesus doll]

Narr   Now Emmanuel is with us,
        Christmas is forever true.
        In your home if you'll invite him,
        God with you and you and you.
            [Hold up Jesus doll]

        God on Earth and God in heaven,
        God with every human heart.
        Greatest gift that e'er was given:
        We and God no more apart.

All   Shout with us the Christmas story.
        Let all heaven and Earth declare:
        Jesus came to Earth from glory,
            [all shout together]
        God Is With Us – Everywhere!

A Christmas Sonnet

Prophetic visions since the world began
(so far before salvation's human birth)

would speak of God's tremendous loving plan
for heav'n to touch the long-estrangèd earth.

Those ancient words at last began to be
in flesh and skin and bone and blood unfurled

In maiden womb and half-made family –
so heaven stooped to touch a fallen world.

Amongst the stable beasts behind the inn,
the baby's eyes saw first a loving mother;

even though their world was full of sin,
yet heav'n touched earth for each in one another.

Now we can cry for peace, goodwill to men,
and for God's heaven to touch his earth again.

Ally Barrett

About the Author

Hi, I'm Fay.

In no particular order I am a mum, mathematician, tea bibber, author, blogger, knitter, theology researcher, children's worker and mad scientist.

I write The Reflectionary, a weekly blog of varied lectionary-based resources for churches, youth groups, children's work and schools' ministry. Popular items are the crafts, all-age worship material, printables and drama scripts.

Everything is free, so pop along and help yourself at www.reflectionary.org. You can sign up there to have the posts sent straight to your mail box. No spam ever, I promise!

I'm also a graduate theology student at Wesley House, Cambridge, currently researching in children's spirituality. You can find links to my published academic works at www.fayrowland.co.uk.

When not writing or studying, I teach maths for a living and spend most of the rest of the time being creative. I worship at a large Anglican church in the English midlands, where I'm part of the teams for all-age worship and Messy Church.

I live with my children and pet dragon in an untidy house full of noise and glue sticks and mess (which I blame on the kids, but really, it's me).

Other Publications

A Bucketful of Ideas for Church Drama

(The Green One)

"Funny, punny, expository and engaging."

"Parables as Jesus would have told them – witty, punchy and thought-provoking."

A(nother) Bucketful of Ideas for Church Drama

(The Blue One)

Including CRISP-tingle, a pop-up nativity, Abraham and his sat-nav, Jonah-Man, the pants prophet, and lots more.

Walking to Bethlehem

An Advent Journey

25 imaginative devotions for adults and children, with reflective colouring and craft ideas.

Top bestseller in Amazon's Advent devotions!

The Big Story

The Bible as a Connected Story for Lent and Holy Week

Through the story from creation to the cross. Amazon's #1 Best-Seller in Bible Meditations!

Printed in Great Britain
by Amazon

48138956R00031